SHOAH NEVER AGAIN

To Adam
your heart will touch the
world and your smile will
own it.
        Love & peace

            2013

SHOAH NEVER AGAIN

THE
JEWISH HOLOCAUST
EXPERIENCE AND SELECTED
POEMS

BY

JAMES E. WHITE JR.

JIM WHITE ENTERPRISES
© 2006 ALL RIGHTS RESERVED
P.O. Box 7701 Beverly Hills, CA 90212
Phone: (310) 271-2960,
E-mail: jimwhiteen@aol.com
www.shoahbooks@aol.com

ISBN 0-9778149-1-2

DEDICATION

I dedicate this book to my dear mother, Ora L. White, and my late father James E. White Sr. You gave me continuous love and helped cultivate my heart, mind, body, and soul. I also would like to say to Dior, Raquel, Brittany, and Maya—I love you more than words could ever convey. To Marcy, Gema and Luz—thanks for my special gifts. To Antoine and Nathan—stay strong sons. To my sisters Tanya, Robin, Geraldmonise, and their children— your presence breeds joy inside of me. To Abdul "Duke" Fakir of the legendary Four Tops—you are the best big brother anyone could ever have. Thank you, Uncle Dan Honigman, for always being there for me. Thanks to Seymour Floyd, my right hand man. To Gene Viglione—I will never forget you pops. To Glenda Sorto—you will always be my one of a kind friend. To Charles Mohr—thank you good friend and teacher. To Patty Santana—for all the many years of support. Most of all I thank you, Jehovah God, for my precious life here on earth.

INTRODUCTION

History has proven, from Biblical days to the current time, that man's instincts are often less than laudable. Man's desire to dominate his fellow man has transcended the ages. This propensity has been evident from the time of the pharaohs in Egypt through the Crusades of the Middle Ages to the ethnic cleansing in the Balkans, the Congo, Sudan, and Rwanda in our day. This human epidemic of terror is precipitated by seeds of greed, intolerance or differences in religious views. No matter what one's religious preference, whether or not we believe in one true God, it is likely that every human being is motivated by his conscience to be fair and just. Animals, on the other hand, having no conscience, are incapable of having true love and have no conception of fairness or justice. Animals are motivated by survival instincts, not love or passion. For example, the humanlike affection your dog pays to you when you come home is not an act of love, but rather a routine that supports its instinct for survival. These are simply beastly instincts, unlike God's generous gift to mankind, the conscience. By that we mean the ability to distinguish right from wrong, justice from injustice, humanity from inhumanity. Take an atheist, for instance. He or she does not have to be taught to have love for his or her parents or children; it's simply a natural component of being human.

We like to think that we tend to exist in a natural state, free of prejudice or bias. Some individuals, however, are motivated more by animallike instincts, seemingly devoid of conscience. Their thirst for power or their interest in their own personal, selfish, and often diabolical agendas overwhelms any natural or God-given sense of conscience and goodwill. History is replete with examples of those who have forsaken God's gift of love and humanity for the lower, more basic animallike instincts that are principally selfish in nature. This infamous club of individuals who have wielded their power relentlessly and unscrupulously would include the likes of Stalin, Slobodan Milosevic, Mussolini, and Idi Amin, to name a few. Some way, somehow, their God-given gift for love and fairness gave way to their animalistic instinct.

There is no greater example of this abhorrent behavior than that of the infamous Nazi leader, Adolf Hitler. What he did to millions of people, Jews and non-Jews alike, the world is just now realizing. I must admit that it was not until I witnessed part of this devastation through watching the Academy Award-winning film *Schindler's List* that I realized the extent of horror thrust upon a generation of innocent people. Having had my own ancestors brought down by slavery, it was easy for me to be sensitive to this issue. But it wasn't until I saw *Schindler's List* that I realized the sameness of the suffering. *Schindler's List* motivated me to research more about why this campaign of terror was perpetrated, as was slavery, on a people so undeserving of its carnage.

One may ask, "How did your understanding of the Holocaust, slavery and other injustices to mankind result in an artistic body of work?" The simple fact is that I was driven by sheer, unrelenting passion to write from my heart what my mind could barely decipher. The more I learned about Hitler's cruelty on such a large and institutional level, the more I felt compelled to write in the one way that I know best, that is, through poetry. Many of these instances, such as slavery, were more personal to me than others. However, I haven't felt anything that resembled this intensity of passion since viewing the epic television saga *Roots*.

My writings are also a product of the knowledge that I have gained through close friendships with Holocaust survivors and their family members. There aren't enough ways to express the hurt they feel from losing a generation of friends and loved ones. It was my desire to illustrate not only the tragedy of a people, but also what survivors and their families had prior to the Holocaust. The abundance of love between women and men, the joys of raising children, the prosperity gained in business and careers, and the desire to make contribution to the world itself. This book of poems, I felt, was the very least that I could do, in memory of all the fallen ones.

James E. White Jr.

TABLE OF CONTENTS

Introduction

Holocaust Poems

SHOAH NEVER AGAIN

A man spends his whole life giving all that he can
To his mother, father, sister, brother,
Wife, children and friends.

He never thought there were those
Who would seek to make him cry,
Then take away his freedom, and plot to see him die.

One by one, life after life, as if we didn't count,
We worked as slaves, we kings and queens
Six million Jews stamped out.

His proud people, brought down by force
And pushed into the wind,
Waited for God to save them from this dreadful, wicked sin.

Schindler's List was just a few,
When we think of the family we had,
If evil men had chosen love, instead of going mad.

But never again will we be made to slave for any man,
We're on our guard, we'll do our part
Our future we must defend.

Once again we've found the strength to build and carry on,
To raise our kids, to teach them well
Show them the world's their home.

Must we forgive, yet never forget
The dark, deep hell we've been
Together we'll stand and vow for life that Shoah, no never again.

About Enemies of Humanity

Terrorists train in destruction every day around the world. They are encouraged by people of all ages who support their cause–to torture and kill anyone who appears to be different. Even to this day, we are reminded of this threat by the presence of groups such as the Ku Klux Klan and other militant rightist groups and militias. Terrorists are also enabled by those who choose to forget or deny occurrences like the Holocaust. We must never forget or become immune or insensitive to this point of view as was witnessed by Prince William's regrettable wearing of a Nazi uniform at a costume party. Sometimes to forget is to allow it to happen again, even if indirectly.

ENEMIES OF HUMANITY

Many would try and have us believe
That man should have no limits
That the First Amendment
Yes, freedom of speech
Could never be anti-Semitic
And crimes that happened long ago
Should be left in the past
And the hurt we feel for lost loved ones
Shouldn't forever last
The men who killed without remorse
Against God's own humanity
Six million Jews in the coldest of blood
Proved their deepest insanity
And don't even think for a moment
These crimes couldn't happen again
Some teach their kids before they can walk
That hate is not a sin
So it's up to us, to use our power
With one voice let's find a way
To fight for our lives and for those we've lost
On this Remembrance Day

About Memories of Courage

The Jewish Holocaust was among history's most cold-blooded tragedies. From the attempted extermination of the American Indians to the execution of Armenian Christians in Muslim Turkey, the slaughtering of whole peoples represented hatred, greed, and indifference to humankind. When you hear of war-torn countries, it's easy to become complacent and insensitive until it happens in your own backyard. The recent 9/11 tragedy hopefully has reminded America, as the leading world power, to never turn a blind eye to terrorism and despotism and to stand vigilant against them. I know that for Americans it is impossible to rescue every country undergoing severe persecution, but there is never an excuse to sit back and do nothing when hundreds of thousands and maybe millions are perishing. Unpopular decisions to save lives sometimes take the utmost of courage.

MEMORIES OF COURAGE

One beautiful day in America
We faced the greatest test
When terror struck Lady Liberty
Leaving wounds upon her breast

Memories of our forefathers
Who made this country great
Drove every man and woman to protect the United States

Six million Jews not long ago
Were our wake-up call
To stand brave one by one
Knowing all could fall
Such memories of courage
Were fought against the beast
While praying to almighty God
To one day live in peace.

What will you do? The time is now
Will your future succumb
To radicals in holy wars
By using human bombs
Will memories or your courage
Minimize the loss
Of blood, love, and dignity
With no more Holocaust?

About The Greatest Ghetto of All

Established in July of 1942, Treblinka was one of three death camps built especially for Operation Reinhard, the killing of all the Jews in Poland. People were put on trains and transported to Treblinka. The security en route was the tightest anyone had seen. Anyone making the camp was beaten with clubs and rifle butts. Upon arrival, men and women were separated. The women were ordered to disrobe and were escorted to the "bathhouses," a term used by the Nazis in deceiving their prisoners as they marched instead straight into gas chambers. By the time the camp was dismantled the following year, it is estimated that nine hundred thousand lives were lost there. The number of known survivors who were held at Treblinka is under forty.

The first thought that came to my mind when I first read about Treblinka was that even though the Nazis had relative power with their guns and other weapons, they still feared the Jews deep down inside. If they didn't fear them, they would not have felt the need to camouflage their intentions. It was through trickery and deceit, backed by the force of arms, that the Germans masterminded this diabolical plot against humanity in many cities across Europe. In Treblinka, they created the greatest ghetto of all.

THE GREATEST GHETTO OF ALL

The Pale Sun Hides Our Frozen Roofs
Seven Hundred Acres Guarded By Those Nazi Wolves
Their Ghetto Prison Our State of Isolation
Four Hundred Thousand Jews Enough To Start A Nation

It's The 1940s And Confusion In The Air
Domination and humiliation We Live In Despair
We Muddle Through Days With One Stolen Glance
They Promise Us Life But We Have No Chance

Our Journey To Treblinka The Blackest Of Days
The Devil's Machinery It's Warsaw We Crave
Infants And Elders A Mass Execution
Rising Up From Few The Only Solution

We Look At The Pictures And Imagine The Stench
Tears Roll From Our Nostrils Our Souls Have Been Lynched
Ignore Not The Writing That Covers The Walls
It Could Happen Again
The Greatest Ghetto Of All

About Good-bye My Child

As trains of prisoners from all over Europe arrived at
Auschwitz, the selection process was immediate. Children
and women formed one large column while men stood in
another. At once, under the supervision of mass murderer
Dr. Josef Mengele, doctors handpicked children who were fit
to work, and others who became Mengele's experimental
guinea pigs. Children under ten or those disabled were sent
immediately to the death camps, declared unfit to live.
Think of the millions of children today who are nursed back
to health because of modern medicines or simple care from a
physician. Could we tolerate the thought of putting these
innocent young people to death because they were not
healthy on one particular day?

GOOD-BYE MY CHILD

How does one say good-bye to a child
Who you've nurtured right from birth
The fact that he's under teenage years
Couldn't possibly diminish his worth
With your future in such uncertainty
And the air so filled with fumes
The guards shout out, children step aside
As they march them closer to the doom
You scream out frantically good-bye, my child
Knowing there's no good to come
There, sadly in his confused little eyes
He knows it's hopeless to run
So breathless you shout, good-bye my child
As he vanishes into the smoke
Another dead Jew, no, more than that
My child, my heart, our hope

About Shaved My Head

Upon arrival at Auschwitz, all men and women were forcibly shaved by prisoners who had been barbers or hairdressers in their earlier lives. Men's heads and beards were shaved with dull razors. Women's hair was clipped close to the skull, while their armpit and other body hair were removed. This was a way to strip all prisoners of their identity in addition to tattooing a number on their left forearm. This practice made me think of Samson during the biblical days and how his power was vanquished with the cutting of his hair. When a person is disfigured or his personal appearance altered so that he becomes generic in appearance, it is a way of stripping him of his dignity and making him invisible in that society. Therefore, the Nazis became the true barbers of death.

SHAVED MY HEAD

You stripped my crown
My symbol of days
My spirit brought down
Your well-planned phase
My hair was my roof
My shield from the sun
Cut strand by strand
With threats from your gun
You shaved my head
My image attacked
Your plan didn't work
God's grown it back
My dignity you took
Till nothing was left
Your shop is now closed
You barbers of death

About My Pants Down

The story of Andrew Stevens is not an extraordinary one as the Jewish experience goes. In the underground resistance movement in Hungary, many were helped. Stevens and others were provided with false identification papers. One day, just like any other man not wearing a uniform, Stevens was stopped by Nazi patrol officers who demanded, as part of the id process, to see if he was circumcised. Had he not shown the counterfeit papers, Stevens would have been shot to death. In addition, if he had opened his pants to reveal his having been circumcised, it would have meant sudden death. It is one thing to read about a horrible event and still another to hear it from the horse's mouth. When my friend Andrew told me about his personal experience, it sent chills through my whole body as I thought of the fact that he was just a single button away from death. Our religious beliefs should be the basis for hope and inspiration, not the harbinger of death.

MY PANTS DOWN

My pants down
Is this a joke?
Pointing their guns
Easily provoke
Your pants down
We want to see
If you are a Jew
Yes a filthy
It means my life
Could be my death
I must think fast
No time is left
I must say more
I must buy time
I cannot show
I'm circumcised
My papers sir
Yes counterfeit
Be on your way
I've escaped death's pit

About Stars and Stripes

As new prisoners undressed for inspection at the camps, their clothes were taken from them and stored in warehouses. Their jewelry, coats, and shoes were sorted by other prisoners, while the newcomers were forced into striped uniforms made of rough cotton. Colored triangles used to identify the "category" of prisoner were placed over a yellow triangle on the uniform to form the six-pointed Star of David. The freedom to work and make or shop for one's clothing is a basic right. It helps us to show our own personality and image. It's the same as the way each face is distinguished from another. It gives us a feeling of independence and uniqueness, the freedom to dream about our future.

STARS AND STRIPES

Yellow stars and dirty stripes
My Jews were forced to wear
Like Samson and Delilah prove
Some pride was in our hair
Barbed wire fence concentration camp
Like an animal in a cage
Yellow stars and dirty stripes
It's hard to hold my rage
Why has God forsaken us
I must not think like that
It's easy to forget one's faith
When you're living life like rats
Stars and stripes forever
Have strengthened my resolve
I encourage every living Jew on earth
To stop and get involved

About Cattle Cars

The first deportation to the camps took place from the Polish ghetto of Zamosc beginning in the spring of 1942. Approximately three thousand men, women, and children were dragged from their homes. Those who attempted to hide were discovered in sewers, cupboards, chimneys, and holes dug in the ground. Families were separated and never saw each other again. Imagine the confusion of this horrible scene. People must have felt their hearts beating rapidly out of control. Panic had to set in as the realization became clearer that something evil was happening and that no one among them had an answer to the predicament they were in. This anxiety must have increased to unbearable proportions as the victims were herded into packed, unventilated animal boxcars.

CATTLE CARS

The cattle cars were small and cramped
Squeaky and cold, dark and damp
The trip that had no return
Its only purpose, to gas and burn
A single hole to peep out of
Left behind the ones we loved
Appropriately named the death trip
They promised us soup for our damaged lips
Reflecting on when our lives were fine
We broke bread together, and drank good wine
Now bellies are sick
And we cannot sleep
It's the leftover smell
From herds of beast
Cattle cars that bump and swerve
The journey of death we didn't deserve

About The Glass Door

Even before Nazi Germany established ghettos and concen-
tration camps, Jews were steadily stripped of their powers.
Their businesses and shops were destroyed; their books were
burned; they were expelled from all military and civil service
positions; and Jewish students were forbidden to study in
German schools. Soon, all Jews were forbidden to leave
Germany because the Reich sought to destroy their entire
race. If we had only known. Few were able to warn us. It
was hard to believe all that the few who were able to get out
were saying. The enemies of these defenseless people were
allowed to take all they had and loved. Most of the world
just looked on, uninformed or uninterested.

THE GLASS DOOR

The enemy was watching
Every move we made
Our progress made them nervous
They wanted us in our graves
They thought that Jewish people
Could take over the world
They hunted and they harvested us
Like oyster losing pearls
Our glass door was shattered
We knew not whom to trust
Jews weren't prepared to fight
And no one protected us
Now the times have changed
Our door is made of steel
Our guards are never down
Our victory is God's will.

VOICES
(A Young Jewish Girl's Story)

I hear voices now; no, I'm not insane
The weakened cries of terror surge
Burned bodies like acid rain
The voice of my father
Would make me feel so safe
My first day of womanhood
Mother teaches, no disgrace
My tears have overshadowed
The glow upon my cheek
The dead marching voices shout
Keep up they'll shoot the weak
My grandparent's voices
Keep ringing in my head
I can't see their faces
Because they all are dead

About Our Things

All prisoners of concentration camps were stripped of their personal belongings as soon as they stepped off the train. All the material taken from the Jews was carefully saved for Germany's use. Money, gold, and most other valuables were sorted first and sent to a special account in the main German bank. Clothes were sold to civilian relief organizations. Even the women's hair was collected, cleaned, and sewn into goods for the Nazi army. Reparations, yes. Reconciliation. Apologies. Acknowledgment from some that it ever happened, when?

OUR THINGS

Our things, what will become of our things?
The years of intelligent planning
Our future from the start
The backbreaking work we did
Dedication from the heart
Our precious family heirlooms
Thrown into a pile
You rummage through our personal things
Ignore our past, how foul
Our things, our things, give us back our things
You'll hang by the ropes, to highest courts
Till you give us back our things

LOST BROTHER OF MINE

My dearest brother, I can't believe my eyes
I haven't seen you since the Nazi uprise
Every day I prayed to see your face
Hitler's army failed to stamp out our race
Remember the days when we laid by the sea
If our sister had lived, how old would she be
You're a little frail, but you still look good
I've aged a bit, and thus I should
Now let's go and look for our mother and dad
Bad news of our brother will make them very sad
Here, please take my hand, like when we were kids
Let's look for our home, just over that ridge
You haven't said a word, for Heaven's sake
Oh! Forgive me dear sir, I've made a terrible mistake.

AN ALIBI OF IGNORANCE

You deprive me of my civil rights
My inheritance you defame
Economic life has turned to dust
Made impossible to sustain
Divide and conquer your master plan
And finally extermination
Forced to wear a yellow star
Yes identity annihilation
It's the 1940s and the Nazi route
Points away from Palestine
The glass house some Jews live in
Is architectural intervention divine
Will history simply repeat itself
The politics of genocide
Not if the resistance fighter in you
Remembers millions died
An alibi of ignorance
The suppression of knowledge a sin
A holocaust in our lifetime?
We won't let it happen again

YIDDISH

Our own little language
Just among ourselves
Grandma spoke it often
Taking food from her shelves
In her own little language
She'd gossip with her friends
She wasn't discriminatory
About women or about men
When the deepest family secrets
Were quietly discussed
She pulled us very close to her
And shared it with deep trust
Yiddish is our blessing
With that funny little sound
It's important to our heritage
We'd be wise to pass it down.

About ORT

In the name of independence, the Organization For Rehabilitation Through Training was founded in 1880 to emancipate underprivileged and uprooted Jewish people. ORT was established by a women's group to train and educate those who were unable to support themselves. A massive organization today, ORT continues to serve approximately 270,000 people each year living in over 100 countries. The self-sufficiency of the Jewish people resurfaced after the war with the help of the ORT. It has inspired the less fortunate to overcome many of the hardships of life that they were simply born into.

ORT

Give me independence
The way life used to be
Let me learn valuable skills
I'll master it you'll see
I never wanted a handout
Hard work is what I love
Allow me to have ownership
Success is in my blood
I've lived through concentration camps
Been called all sorts of names
ORT restored my dignity
For you, ORT can do the same.

ONE RABBI

He pulled them from the gas chambers
After their little lives were taken
He worried not of consequence
Blessing all of the forsaken
One by one he carried them out
Each child he dearly cradled
God's little Jews had no chance
Our greatest promise made fatal
No one dared to stop Rabbi
As he leaned to kiss just one
This fearless man prayed as if
The enemy had never won
Later that day he turned to us
And said, my children feel no blame
They'll never answer to a number again
We'll remember them all by name

About The Once Chosen Ones

In the early years of Christianity and in recent times, Jews were called Christ killers, murderers of God. It is believed that Martin Luther, the founder of Protestantism, declared they were one of Christianity's most vicious enemies. Violence against Jewish people escalated during his lifetime in the 1500s and would continue for centuries. But very few talk about there being a time when Jews were selected as God's chosen people, and Jesus was himself a Jew. No nation of people should be persecuted forever for something a few did back in biblical days. The Creator forgives all of us every minute of each day for our sins against his will, so who are we to continue to pass judgment on others?

THE ONCE CHOSEN ONES

In the biblical days
Jewish life wasn't fun
God allowed persecution
As it was with his Son
No more was allowed
Than they could daily bear
And when some complained
God's love was still shared
Once out of the wilderness
Their lives were truly blessed
As for Shoah survivors today
God will do nothing less
So tell the Bible stories
To your daughters and your sons
And daily remind them of
God's once chosen ones

ISRAEL

I long to see my Israel
The land that I so love
Its fabric-woven people
Bring olive branch and dove
Its loving peace with neighbors
Is never far remote
I believe in my heart of hearts
That is my nation's vote
I cherish you my Israel
I will cry my last tear
To walk among your chosen ones
And travel in you without fear

DREAM

Wake me up in the morning
I so look forward to
I pray no bad dreams follow me
My heart cries for a new
I only close my eyes at night
To wipe my canvas clean
And paint a better portrait than
The tortures in this dream
I play roulette deep in my mind
As sunlight hits my face
I know the world will rescue me
Before there is no trace.

LOOK FOR ME

Look for me my love
With the rising of each sun
I will never cease to look for you
Even when this war is done
I'll never forget the plans we made
That we'd live near the sea
Go to sleep with waves that flow
And raise our family
I once heard a poet say
That lives were meant to be
I'll always look for you my love
Don't ever stop looking for me.

About Underground

Credited with saving one hundred thousand Hungarian Jews from persecution, Raoul Wallenberg was a successful Swedish businessman. He first handed out real Schutz passes (protective documents), accepted by both Germans and Hungarians as signs of an official connection with neutral Sweden during the war. Acquiring thirty houses in which Jews lived, Wallenberg influenced other representatives of neutral nations to open safe houses. My friend Andrew Stevens first brought to my attention the heroic group of people who followed Raoul Wallenberg's example and took unbelievable chances to save lives, the most active group being the underground Zionist youth movement. Despite the fact that they didn't have the appropriate tools, they took whatever they could find and pieced together documents that were sufficient enough to fool even the trained eye.

UNDERGROUND

Now you see us now you don't
We refuse to be your slave
We escape the hands of death
To look for lives to save
Underground from light to dark
Inconspicuously fight the war
Helping all the Jews we can
Their cries we'll not ignore
Following the steps of Wallenberg
Heaven sent this Swede
He gave life-giving documents to Hungarian refugees
This heroic Swedish diplomat passed the highest test
Confronted enemies face to face and saved Jews in Budapest

About My Brother's Keeper

Jona and Avram give meaning to the expression "my brother's keeper." After days of hiding from the Nazis, Jona and Avram Goldrich were able to escape their hometown of Turka, Poland. Through forest and mountains, city to city, they journeyed from Budapest to Palestine with the help of a few. Years later, the Goldrich brothers would be credited for aiding refugees in Israel. There are many stories of survival and human determination. This just happens to be one about a friend of mine. I have met very few men who on a daily basis show his love for his people like Jona Goldrich. From the United States to Tel Aviv, he never forgets where he came from. He, like many others, gives each and every day of his life, time, money, and voice to help others in need.

MY BROTHER'S KEEPER

I was just fourteen when we left our home
The Germans occupied Turka and happy days were gone
A population of 5,000 was reduced to 2,000 that year
And I, Jona, and my brother Avram lived constantly in Nazi fear
Our family made a decision before it was all too late
It broke two little boys' hearts to find that their family
would soon separate
A guide was hired to smuggle us to Munkateh, Hungary
He was to only get paid in full when we were safe and free
My father and I devised a plan that wasn't at all Kiddish
A note that proved our safe arrival was written down in Yiddish
We traveled mountains, woods, and trains;
it proved to be hard work
Our father paid for our precious lives from the
diamonds sewn in our shirts
From Budapest to Palestine I held my brother's hand
By the 1950s we both realized that two boys became all man
Now Avram's in Israel and I'm in the U.S. our love's
grown only deeper
Because we never forgot how important it was to remain our
brother's keeper.

About If You Will It, It Is No Dream

Hungarian journalist and playwright Theodor Herzl invented Zionism, the plight for a Jewish state in Palestine, in hopes of obtaining social equality for all in 1896. With this thought in mind for equality and independence, Herzl was prompted to write, "If you will it, it is no dream." Herzl died before an estimated six million Jews were killed during the Holocaust. The Jewish founders of Tel Aviv had little more to work with than their own backs and camels. In 1936, members of the Zif-Zif gravel cooperative were moving sand and rock from the beach by camel caravan to concrete manufacturing sites in the process of building a city. Long before there was a state, the building blocks were laid by the sweat of a people determined to live on their own land, be self reliant, and live in peace. Herzl also said, "Let the sovereignty be granted us over a portion of the globe large enough to satisfy the rightful requirements of a nation; the rest we will manage for ourselves."

This history of Tel Aviv was especially inspiring to me because it demonstrated what could be accomplished when the dream of one man is embraced by a dedicated people having faith in the creator who can make miracles happen with a grain of sand.

IF YOU WILL IT, IT IS NO DREAM

We helped build a nation
Although we were few
Took charge of your future
What else could we do
Terrorist, politics
Economy and war
God's love for our people
Would knock down hate's door
If you will it
It's no dream, Theodor said
Tell all of our children
When we put them to bed
Israel forever
Is how it must be
Yes Jews from all nations
And Tel Aviv
If ever you will it
It's certainly no dream
A new century's here
The slate must be clean
We can never get back at any cost
All of the loved ones we tragically lost
All of the guilty
Try and repay
For six million lives
On this Remembrance Day

About Run For My Life

Fortunately there were a small number of brave young Jews who resisted any orders that came from the Nazis, knowing that all these orders would lead to their elimination. They chose to take destiny into their own hands. They refused to follow the order to march with others to the gathering place. Usually it was a brickyard; from there the next step would have been the exterminator in Auschwitz. They–like my friend Andrew–joined in the resistance movement with other brave men, and by using different names and hiding places, they moved around freely. Their activities not only aimed to save their lives, but also to help others with falsified documents. Many Jews were saved from certain death with these documents. Unfortunately, many of them were caught. This poem tells the story of two players. One, who received the documents from Andrew, was caught; he was forced to give away Andrew's identity and his role in the underground. So, Andrew–he is the "rebel with a cause"–was also arrested, but his determination to outfox the enemy saved his own life and gave him time to save others. He saved many lives, so, according to the Talmud: "He saved the world!"

Run For My Life
(As told by Andrew Stevens)

A knock on my door in the middle of the night
Arrested by Nazis too late to take flight
A rebel with a cause I had to save lives
Making false documents for husbands and wives
They tortured my friend until he gave up my name
Then dumped him down river him I never blamed
We're taking you in you'll die by the gun
I had to distract them attack them and run
There is the Jew from windows they screamed
My heart pumping fast out of body it seemed
Bullets are blazing the streets of Budapest
In a telephone booth I hid and to rest
Eluding the soldiers I sent on my way
Shot in the ankle just another life-saving day

Freedom and Tolerance Poems

About Innocence Lost

Jews were forced into ghettos temporarily before they were transported to concentration camps. The overcrowding of eight to fifteen to a room sent many outside to join the sick and dying that were already there. Fed as little as 220 calories each day, countless children, whose parents had already died of starvation or disease, huddled in the streets. These events are never to be forgotten, lest they happen again. When dictators and outlaw leaders persecute portions of their own population and then prohibit assistance from the outside, their design is essentially to eliminate those groups of people from the general population. We have seen this ungodly behavior repeat itself in the City of Good housing project in Rio de Janeiro, Brazil. Although not recognized as a formal policy of the government, officials quietly turned a blind eye as homeless and destitute children were slaughtered in the streets, thereby not interfering with commerce and tourism.

INNOCENCE LOST

Little eyes, little mouths, little hands, little feet
No help from anyone so they live on the street

Is it really their fault their clothes are all dirty
They're hungry and confused heaven knows they're more worthy

No family, no food, no roof overhead
Just a hand from us, or a warm bed
The world must stop looking the other way

If they weren't so frightened, just what would they say
Would they damn political leaders with their political gain?
Or would they be like Jesus and from anger refrain
Just what will it take to abolish their cries
Pure innocence lost, please no more lies

About True Freedom

In May 1939, 930 Jews bought passage to the United States on the S.S. *St. Louis*, but because of the harsh immigration laws, they were not allowed to land in the States as all of their papers were not in order. People like Eleanor Roosevelt and others tried to circumvent the immigration laws by having the ship land in the Virgin Islands, but they were also turned away there. The boat returned them all back to Europe, and most were eventually terminated by the Nazis. This happened three months before the outbreak of the war, and three years before the establishment of the death camps.

TRUE FREEDOM

True freedom
What does it mean
Is it living one's life
The way it is dreamed

Is it leaving a country
Whenever you please
Is it asking for help
But not on your knees

Being constantly told
I shouldn't come here
Where can I belong
And never have fear

The country I had
Is now under siege
And where I live now
Has less of my needs

Where can I go
Who will take me
I've risked my life
On the dangerous sea
Is it because of my race
That they're sending me back
I feel true freedom
Is under attack

WAR AND PEACE

As I looked out the window of a plane
I felt so insignificant,
To see the mountains, the ocean, the vast real estate
I felt God's true magnificence
I wondered how men around the world
Could participate in a war
While right inside this neighborhood
A child plays with a toy.

When God thinks of such a loss of life
It has to make him sad
We've lost our sons to war it's true
But God's the All-Mighty Dad
If it were our choice, we'd end it all
And let man go no further
But God puts up with each of us
Both common man and governor
So let's bow our heads and pray for peace
Help the poor and homeless lives
Because you never know when that beggar you meet
Is All-Mighty God in disguise.

About Our Land

I once heard someone say that if you gave one man all the money in the world, then gave another all the land in the world, the one with the land eventually would end up with all of the money. Land, it appears, is more often than not the main reason for war. But when there is enough for all to live on, why do families have to continue dying for it? This point cannot be lost on the new settlers in Gaza.

OUR LAND

This land is my land
This land is your land
This land is God's land
Mountains dirt and sand
Giving it up I know will be tough
To love and live
And no longer to fuss
We're fighting this war
For a little piece of land
Should we ever try
To deprive any man
Give them their piece
And we shall have ours
Giving them that land
Shows them our true power.

About Free

By the end of 1942 during the Nazi reign, over six thousand labor camps existed in Poland alone. While it is impossible to estimate how many others in the world are enslaved today, it would be accurate to say that there are many who are not free. The Universal Declaration of Human Rights states, "Whereas recognition of the inherent dignity and of the equal and inalienable rights of all members of the human family is the foundation of freedom, justice, and peace in the world, Whereas disregard and contempt for human rights have resulted in human acts that have outraged the conscience of mankind, and the advent of a world in which human beings shall enjoy freedom of speech and belief and freedom from fear and want has been proclaimed as the highest aspirations of a common people." In America, the Constitution and the Declaration of Independence espouse the same virtues of freedom and justice as their mantra.

Let us learn from history that democracy can be accomplished when the word freedom and its true meaning are not watered down.

FREE

Free to look where I please
Go where I please
Think what I please
Eat what I please
Wear what I please
Worship who I please
Work where I please
Say what I please
Love whom I please
But not on my knees
Just free.

About A Time to Stand

Proving that one voice can inspire a nation, Rosa Parks put a human face on the civil rights movement across the United States. In 1955, Parks refused to give up her seat to a white citizen on a bus in Montgomery, Alabama. As a result, leaders, priests, teachers, doctors, and activists everywhere were inspired to risk their lives and to stand up for what they believe in. One might ask, "What does this poem have to do with the Holocaust and the tragedies that occurred during Hitler's reign?" The courageous example of this frail little black woman is universal in its applications to those many defenseless Jewish mothers who tried so desperately to stand up against the tyranny of the Nazi regime, doing whatever it took to survive and keep their families safe. The agony of seeing the strongest image in your life—your father, your husband, your brothers—being diminished down to less than dirt had to be more than any human being should have to experience. But through it all, our Jewish mothers, sisters, and daughters persevered with the little dignity they had left. Despite the odds or the dangers, it was these often little, frail Jewish women who took the many risks that were necessary to keep their spirits and hopes alive. Let's face it, under the day-to-day duress that they endured, the Jewish women of the Holocaust had little time for tears. They set a fine example for today's young women who desire to make a difference.

A TIME TO STAND

I thought about Rosa Parks
And how she must have felt
After working all day long
And finding only one seat left
Yes she paid her bus fare
Just like everyone else
But got treated as if
She was dust on one's shelf
Yet that day the world gained a hero indeed
Because she did stand up
For what she believed
And if that sweet little woman
Hadn't found her way
I'm sure that this man wouldn't be standing here today.
So when I hear anyone making comments that ban
If I value her courage
Then I too must stand.

DIVERSITY

What is a world without diversity?
Would Noah build an ark for only one animal at sea?
An Olympic dream could never be had
If only black and white represented every flag
If all the babies born into the world
Were all little boys because we couldn't have girls
Yes God shows us how much we're adored
By making us different the moment we're born
So look around now and see all the colors
Both yellow and brown all sisters and brothers
So get used to it that's how it should be
A world filled with children, yes with God's Diversity

AND THE WINNER IS…

And the winner is…
The teacher who taught the Golden Rule
The person who prayed in Sunday's school
The firemen who pulled you from the flame
The parent who coached the Little League game
The police who protected us from crime
The guide who led all the blind
The scientist who stamped out polio
The judge who opened freedom's door
The doctor who gave the wonder pill
The soldier who died so we could live
The neighbor who watered your favorite rose
The mother who washed your little clothes
The father who worked both night and day
The God who paved your every way
And the winner is…
You!

Love Poems Section Summary

The biblical definition of love is a criteria of positive parameters that elevates love to a noble but achievable stature. Corinthians 13:4 states, "Love is long-suffering and kind. Love is not jealous, it does not brag, does not get puffed up, does not behave indecently, does not look for its own interests, does not become provoked. It does not keep count of the injury. It does not rejoice over unrighteousness, but rejoices with the truth. It bears all things, believes all things, hopes all things, endures all things."

Love is, in fact, the single thread that binds mankind from one generation to the next. It is the union of hearts and interests that perpetuates the species and provides the foundations from which all societies emanate. It is this glorious triumph of affection and emotions that pushes us forward to endure hardships, to make sacrifices, and to achieve and make accomplishments. Love is the bedrock of family. Love is the one thing that we share with others that isn't dependent on wherewithal, competence, productivity or material worth. Love has survived despite monumental and seemingly insurmountable odds against the likelihood of its existence. But regardless of the consequences, it has endured it all. Nothing has been more illustrative of love's arduous journey through the annals of history than that between the Jews as they struggled to survive life in the work camps and beyond. The relationships that endured created the foundation for a culture to survive and prosper. Their love remained when seemingly all else was taken away. That's why I felt it a necessity to add to this collection of poems, examples of love between men and women, husbands and wives, parents and children, brothers and sisters, and family and friends. Human beings, just like you and me.

MY WIFE

Every time I think I've mastered
All the ways of keeping my cool
I just fall apart
My heart just gets weak for you
It makes me do the things I do for you

With you I feel no pain
Because I have so much more to gain
Being with you every time you speak
You make me reach love's highest peak
And please don't ever stop

With you I feel no pain
Because I have so much to gain
You are my wife
My reason
My song
My life.

OUR LOVE

When I first laid eyes on you
My heart started to move so fast
Far beyond control
And I knew that whoever created you
Felt you should be one of a kind
So he broke the mold

You're so special girl
Please don't get me wrong
My motives aren't just made of lust
I want a love to call my own
I'm just saying what I feel
Our love will come to be
I'll ask you, you'll say I do
We'll both live happily
Our love.

DON'T BREAK MY HEART

I could have sworn I saw you in the night
With someone else you held oh so tight
Was it my eyes playing tricks on me
A part of life I hoped I'd never see
Some other love has torn us apart
I'm so confused oh where do I start
It's too late to put up my guard
Don't break my heart

You don't know what you mean to me
I look in your eyes and they love back at me
Say you'll be with me until eternity
Forever together that would be so right
Our favorite song you holding me so tight
Please don't break my heart.

I'M IN LOVE

I'm in love and I must tell someone
Every time I see your face
I get so warm inside
I ask my mom
I ask my dad
To listen for a while
Then I express how I feel
It's like I'm in a daze
I'm hooked on love
And don't want out
Just keep me in your maze
I'm in love and I must tell someone

It's not really fair
I can't even sleep
Sometimes it's hard for me to eat
I just keep staring into my food
Thinking of you puts me in the mood
I'm in love.

LEAVE WELL ENOUGH ALONE

Every time it all feels right, someone will screw it up.
It's hard enough to find true love, we dare not interrupt.

The body's fine, a heart of gold, best sex you ever had.
But you look for things that shouldn't count, self-sabotage, how sad.

We like it when we're almost there, so afraid to be complete.
We'd rather fall flat on our ass than land up on our feet.

But time ticks on, and life is short, we must make up our minds
To pick fruit from the closest tree, not from the furthest vine.
I know you'll say, it's not my fault," and place blame on others.
But change your ways, or for the rest of your life, you'll live at
home with Mother.

LET ME BE WORTHY

Let me be worthy, I've lived another day
I rose with the sun, felt the warmth of its rays
I bathed in sweet water, 'twas cool to my face
I breathed in fresh air from this Earth you have placed
I hope I am worthy of my family so dear
One look at my children makes your plan so clear
I want to be worthy of the love of my life
Beautiful or strong, husband or wife
I pray that I am worthy of my neighbors and friends
As I ask for forgiveness for all of my sins
Help me be worthy through good times or strife
As I pray to the highest, you creator of life

Friends and Family Poems

MY FRIEND STANLEY

I have a friend named Stanley
And yes, he's loved by all
He sees the good in every man and woman big or small
He's touched so many people's lives
And never looked for praise
He reminds me of the Son of God
Way back in Bible days
He's that brother who you never had
When you're wrong he speaks right up
Sharing words of wisdom true
Never harsh, but a special touch
He laughs at your jokes
And tell other folks how talented you are
And when you need a helping hand
He's never very far
Yes my friend, you're truly blessed
You have an angel's heart
And no matter where you are on earth
We'll never be apart
Rock stars would be envious
If they could see
The crowds you attract
Because you are the greatest friend of all
I love you Stanley Black

GAIL

Try and imagine a flower
That takes your breath away
Or a beautiful majestic angel
Watching over you every day

It's fair to say a man with this
Could never ever fail
Well this pal of mine found such a gift
In his precious wife, dear Gail

For many years, they were best friends
They shared good times and bad
And when she gave him two great kids
He cherished what they had

And if there was ever any doubt
Of how great Gail's love could be
Reflect upon her time with us
It proved she had love's key

So don't be sad, oh pal of mine
Always remember this
Imagine every flower
Is surely Gail's best kiss

When memories of her get a little rough
And sometimes hard to view
That majestic angel with your Gail's face
Is watching over you

MOTHER

Don't be surprised
I turned out this way
Your heart and your hands
Made possible this day
It's because of you mom
That I'm never enslaved
By the grace of God
You've made my roads paved
There were times you fed me
When you had nothing to eat
I wore comfortable shoes
You walked in bare feet
I would give up my life
To erase all of your pain
To see you alive
I have so much to gain
I never wanted
To break your heart
I wish back the moments
That we were apart

SHE'S GROWING SO FAST

She's growing so fast
Oh, what can I do?
She's so independent now
She ties her own shoes
It's breaking my heart
I can't wipe her nose
She's growing so fast
I can't pick her clothes
She's off to college now
And I can't hold her hand

I'm getting really scared
Because I can't choose her man
She planned her own wedding
And gave me one little part
Now she is having a baby
Oh, how I miss that part
I wish I had back
All those precious little times
But she's grown so fast
That little girl of mine

LITTLE ANGEL

One beautiful day in heaven
All were asked to join
To witness something special
The cutest angel born
Most angels were all white
And flew around the air
But Elaine was sent to earth
Because of her red hair
Her little heart was broken
She had to hide her wings
The world quickly learned
The love Elaine would bring
A devoted wife and mother
Was really her disguise
Because making others happy
Was truly God's surprise
So let's send her our best wishes
On her very special night
Because she can't go back to heaven
Until her hair's completely white

Famous People Section Summary

Television, film, literature, and the Internet have become the world's magnifying glass and a barometer for success. Many Jewish people who were affected by the Holocaust through their ancestry just happen to be famous. These celebrities have made a tremendous contribution to the world of multimedia. They've become particularly important to society because they can influence opinions or create controversy among millions of people at a time. Jewish entertainment executives and celebrities, through special charities and philanthropy, have worked individually and collectively to promote unity and tolerance on a global basis. Let's face it; what is fame and fortune worth when it cannot save lives? That's why I felt Jews in the entertainment community should be recognized in this collection of poems. Yes, for their creativity and for tactfully reminding people of the past injustices of the Holocaust. What happened to the Jews could have been mirrored by any other religious or ethnic group on earth. The list of Jewish celebrity role models is too vast to recognize them all. I have decided to write about a few who have influenced my life and career.

THE VOICE OF A KING
Dedicated to Larry King

The Ali of broadcasting is what people say
Over forty-five years a King every day
Dark rims and suspenders, tall and good-looking
Millions tune in to see what he's cooking
The master of the microphone ahead of the game
Forty thousand interviews he's in five halls of fame
A political debate or a star on West Wing
They all come to hear the voice of the King
The money he's made did not go to waste
He gave it to charity to continue the race
His friends will all say he's the best they've ever had
To Shawn and the kids he's the world's greatest dad
He enters a room and they all start to lean
To hear what comes out of the mouth of a King
Yes if Ali were here he'd give his best rhyme
He'd say Larry's the greatest, King of all time

About From Steven With Love

Oskar Schindler, an ethnic German businessman living in Czechoslovakia, took over an enamelware company in Poland for the German Army. He arranged to hire Jewish workers to circumvent their deportation to the camps. As Steven Spielberg's film Schindler's List depicts, Schindler was responsible for saving 1,200 lives through bribery and using his connections in Europe. The one part of the film that I am certain will stay with me forever was when it was all over and Hitler had lost and Mr. Schindler was standing before the remaining Jewish factory workers and he suddenly began weeping, saying that he could have done more. One life was too many to lose, but thank God he saved as many as he did.

FROM STEVEN WITH LOVE

When people think of Spielberg
And the magic he creates
He brings out the kid in us
The film world thinks he's great
Whether rubbing elbows with Tom Hanks
Or with Geffen or Katzenberg
This talented son of an engineer
Was determined to be heard
He went from a four hundred dollar loan
To Raiders of The Lost Ark
Once snubbed by some in Hollywood
Then directed Jurassic Park
When A Color Purple lost one year
Yes, Oscar's greatest dis
Steven proved true majesty
When he directed Schindler's List
From that day on his accolades
Could grow tall as the highest steeple
But nothing could be more important than
This great film he gave to Jewish people.

About A Nobel Prize

Today, nearly six million Jews live in the United States. Israel, the Jewish state, has a population of over six million. Many accomplished scholars, writers, musicians, scientists, and politicians are Holocaust survivors or are the relatives of survivors. Speaking out against hate crimes and other injustices, they continue to lead humanitarian efforts globally. Fortunately, the Nazi plan to exterminate the Jewish people failed. Think of the great loss to human society if we had been deprived of the contribution of so many talented Jews. The tragedy is thinking about all of the geniuses and other potential contributors to the advancement of culture and civilization who were lost in the Holocaust.

A NOBEL PRIZE

Ten Nobels in Literature
Eight Nobels in Peace
Twenty-two prizes in Chemistry
All Jews to say the least
Thirteen awards in Economics
The Medicine field was great
Jews led the count with ninety-five
First win in 1908
Thirty-one wins in physics
From Michelson to Einstein
Sometimes two Jews won the same year
Like in 1979
From 1910 to '95
We won 129 times
We're only 0.02 percent of the world
But we've done our part just fine

Queen of Queens
Dedicated to Barbra Streisand

In my search to find a queen
The choices weren't quite vast
I imagined her on a golden throne
Her greatness forever last
I've been in the presence of so-called queens
But I couldn't feel their hearts
Because to love the people then yourself
Is how queeens get their start
That special style we try to have
A queen shows effortless
And from New York City to Paris, France
Queen Streisand you're the best
Some eighty gold and platinum albums
Your walls are covered with
Surpassing the Beatles and Rolling Stones
Second to only Elvis no myth
Ten Golden Globes a Cecille DeMille
An Oscar for Funny Girl
First to produce, write, and direct
From a female star in the world
Your accolades are far too many
To write all of them down
But don't ever think that a day goes by
When we don't marvel your great crown

Acknowledgments

I would like to thank the following friends of mine for their encouragement and support. Rabbi Marvin Hier, Stanley Black, Jona Goldrich, Leo David, Andrew Stevens, Lawrence N. Field, Larry King, Marvin Rothenberg, Nate Shapell, Irving Katzef, Chaim Mintz, Mark Freidman, Marty Apec, David Entin, Yoal Hasson, Charles Dezengof, Max Webb, Fred Moss, Dave Smith, Bob Stern, Jerry Oren, Yoav Peled, Candi Cross, Rabbi Abraham Cooper, Maurice Pechman, Joyce Moss, Morrie Steinberg, and Jack Heller. And last but not least, I would like to thank all of the Holocaust survivors and their families all over the world.